Original title:
The Apple's Whisper

Copyright © 2025 Creative Arts Management OÜ
All rights reserved.

Author: Tobias Winslow
ISBN HARDBACK: 978-1-80586-301-4
ISBN PAPERBACK: 978-1-80586-773-9

Gleaning Hidden Insights

In the orchard's heart, a secret chat,
A squirrel in shades, wearing a hat.
He juggles his acorns, quite the show,
While the winds giggle softly below.

Near the tree trunk, a worm takes a peek,
Saying, "I'm wise, but kind of oblique!"
He spins tales of dreams rather absurd,
Like riding on clouds or flying a bird.

A crow cackles loudly, "What's the fuss?"
Pondering life, squeezed in a bus.
Branches rustle with mischievous glee,
As the fruit rolls down, laughing with me.

In this chaos, there's wisdom to find—
A giggle of nature, oh so unconfined!
So gather around for a chuckle or two,
And glean all the laughs from the trees, just for you!

Far Beneath the Skin

In a tree of green, a joke was spun,
An apple claimed, it was the chosen one.
It danced with glee, swaying to and fro,
While worms below said, "We're the stars of the show."

The leaves shook hard, in laughter they swayed,
As squirrels chimed in, their nutty charades.
The fruit argued back, with a crispy zing,
"But I'm the one who gets the bling after spring!"

The Silent Courtship

Two fruits did flirt, on the branch so high,
A peach blushed pink, with a twinkle in its eye.
The apple just grinned, with a rosy delight,
And whispered sweet dreams in the soft moonlight.

The pears rolled their eyes, on the line below,
"You think you're so cute, with your vibrant glow?"
But the apple just chuckled, with zest in its heart,
"It's all about style, you're just pie charts!"

Symphony of Orchard Lives

In the orchard's midst, a wild concert grew,
With bees on the mic, buzzing a tune anew.
The apples clapped backs, with peels peeled wide,
While the grapes all laughed, out of sheer pride.

The carrots in rows, tried to join the beat,
But their roots got tangled, no chance to compete.
As tomatoes rolled in, red-faced and round,
They joined the jam session, in laughter profound.

Lifting Nature's Veil

A prank was afoot, in the orchard's breath,
The apples conspired, a scheme 'til death.
They'd drop from the tree, with a resounding thud,
And giggle as humans splashed in the mud.

The cider was bubbling, with laughs all around,
As critters joined in, a sweet symphony sound.
With careful precision, they orchestrated fun,
A jest in the air, till the day was done.

Golden Orchard Whispers

In a grove where sunlight plays,
The fruit wears coats of sunny rays.
Each little bite, a giggle shared,
With laughter ripe, no one is scared.

Silly squirrels dance around,
Chasing shadows on the ground.
As breezes tease the branches high,
Each fruit just winks, oh my, oh my!

Beneath the Boughs of Quietude

Beneath the boughs, a secret schemes,
As apples fake their juicy dreams.
They roll and tumble, full of glee,
Wishing to be free, oh me!

A worm confesses with a laugh,
"I'm just here for the juicy half!"
With every crunch, the orchard sighs,
They giggle softly, oh, what a prize!

Secrets Cradled in Juicy Flesh

Inside this fruit, a tale unfolds,
Of all the mischief that it holds.
With every bite, a secret's burst,
In juicy flesh, the giggles thirst.

A core of laughs, a heart of fun,
Wormy whispers from everyone.
Each nibble brings a juicy jest,
In orchard's heart, we find our fest!

A Vineyard's Quiet Confession

In vineyards green, where grapes do hang,
The sweetest laughs, the joy they sang.
Beneath the leaves, a joke is cracked,
As nature smiles, it just attracts.

A grape once tripped, fell on its face,
Now bounces back with extra grace.
The vines all giggle, swaying wide,
In juicy fields, the jokes abide!

Fruit of Secrets

In a garden where laughter plays,
Cherries giggle in sunny rays.
Bananas hide their silly grins,
While oranges dance, making spins.

Peaches gossip in fruity tones,
As pears share tales of silly moans.
Lemons roll with jokes so bright,
Under the stars, they laugh at night.

Echoes in the Orchard

Granny Smith sings a tune so sweet,
While apricots juggle, skipping their feet.
All the berries join in a chorus,
Their voices mix, causing a ruckus.

Grapes laugh as they tumble down,
Wearing their juice like a silly crown.
Every fruit shares a joke or two,
In this orchard of joy, nothing feels blue.

Beneath the Crimson Skin

Under scarlet skin, a joke lies hid,
A secret's shared; oh, how they kid!
With tiny seeds that burst out in glee,
Each bite reveals their comedy.

Lurking beneath the sweet facade,
Lemons' laughter is never marred.
So take a bite, don't miss the fun,
Fruit-filled jests for everyone!

Sweet Confidences

In a quiet grove where fruits confide,
Kiwi whispers secrets, with pride.
Raspberries chuckle, spilling a laugh,
As peaches tease with their juicy half.

A slice of fruit, a friend to share,
Tales of silliness fill the air.
With every crunch, joy is released,
A fruity gathering, the funniest feast!

Voices in the Shade

In the quiet of the trees, they chat,
Fruits in a chorus, imagine that!
An orange sings, a banana grins,
While lemons roll their eyes in spins.

A pear tells jokes, so ripe and round,
While melons laugh, making silly sounds.
The cherry's blush, a giggling spree,
In the shade of humor, wild and free.

The Secret Garden's Breath

In a nook where secrets bloom and play,
The berries giggle in a cheeky way.
A sunflower leans, whispers from above,
Telling tales of fruits in love.

Tomatoes blush, their ripening prank,
While radishes dance in a jolly rank.
The garden breathes with laughter, bright,
As veggies jest 'til the fall of night.

Serendipity Among the Leaves

Amidst the leaves, a party stirs,
With dancing apples, all in a blur.
A kumquat twirls, a figs delight,
While dancing grapes hide out of sight.

The wildest melons roll on the ground,
Where liberation in laughter is found.
They joke about weather, ripe and bold,
Sweet tales of sunshine never grow old.

Choreography of Fruits

Fruits gather 'round for a delightful show,
With a twist, a sway, and a giggling flow.
The apples lead, with a wink and a spin,
While plums get dizzy, ready to grin.

Pineapples rave with their funky style,
While berries bounce in a fruity while.
A harvest dance in joyous parade,
In this jolly scene, sunshine won't fade.

Juicy Confessions

In the orchard where laughter springs,
A creature plots with tiny wings.
He steals a slice, just one, oh please,
Chasing dreams beneath the trees.

A juicy truth, he can't resist,
From the core, he takes a twist.
Squirrel chases him, oh what a sight,
Both scamper off, a comical flight.

They share a bite, it's all in fun,
Sticky paws, two under the sun.
Laughter echoes, the world spins round,
In this patch, pure joy is found.

Beneath the Scarlet Skin

A chubby critter, cheeky grin,
Winks at all beneath a skin.
Tickles friends with fruity glee,
Juicy lies and silly spree.

Beneath the scarlet, secrets dwell,
In each bite, a giggle bell.
A bouncing hare joins in the play,
With every munch, they dance away.

The shade invites the laughter spree,
As critters frolic wild and free.
Fables shared with every crunch,
In this slice, it's a funny hunch!

Soft Murmurs in Bloom

In the garden, whispers play,
Petals blush, not far away.
Bees buzz jokes and tickle leaves,
A dance of giggles that never leaves.

Soft murmurs float on gentle air,
A duo of fruits with silly flair.
One says 'Ripe!' and the crowd does cheer,
While others giggle, 'Oh dear, oh dear!'

In each soft laugh, a secret swirls,
A tale of fruits and funny whirls.
Ticklish vines with laughter bound,
In bloom, joyous moments found.

The Temptation's Song

In a grove where shadows prance,
A tempting tune begins to dance.
Fruits hum low, a playful tease,
Making creatures giggle with ease.

A tune of mischief, sweet and bright,
Sings to critters, day and night.
Jumping high with hearts set free,
In the rhythm of silliness, they agree.

A berry chimes, 'Come take a bite!'
While others joke, 'We'll take flight!'
In this orchard of delightful cheer,
Every song pulls laughter near.

Secrets of the Grove

In the grove where giggles grow,
The little fruits put on a show.
A winking pear, a smirking peach,
They work together, not out of reach.

An apple rolled upon the floor,
Cried, "Watch out! I'm not your chore!"
A cherry chuckled, 'Don't you fret,
This vine will catch you, place your bet!'

A grape with dreams of being tall,
Said, "I'm the star, I'll take it all!"
But when the vine began to sway,
He floated down in disarray.

They laugh and play without a care,
Each fruity buddy loves to share.
In this grove where stories bloom,
Find the humor amidst the gloom.

The Enchanted Bite

In a kitchen, magic brews,
With jars of sweets and shiny hues.
A bite of cake, a lollipop,
One taste will make your heart just stop.

A cookie winked with chocolate chips,
And whispered jokes with sugar lips.
Donuts danced in circles wide,
While cupcakes swirled with frosted pride.

But beware the jelly bean's grin,
It might just lead you into sin.
One munch and poof, you start to float,
A sticky, sweet, and funny boat!

So grab a fork and don't be shy,
In this land, the treats can fly.
A laugh, a smile, a cheerful bite,
Makes every day a pure delight.

Whispers of the Harvest Moon

Underneath the harvest glow,
Gourd and squash do steal the show.
A pumpkin dons a silly hat,
And laughs at all the folks like that.

Tomatoes blush in shades of red,
As carrots dance with grinning head.
With every whisper, every cheer,
They share their jokes, oh so sincere.

Corn on cob with kernels bright,
Jokes about the stars at night.
"Why did the apple cross the road?
To tell a joke, lightening the load."

At the harvest moon's bright beam,
The veggies bask in laughter's dream.
When they unite in comic jest,
The night transforms; they are the best!

Lullaby of the Trees

Beneath the swaying branches' sway,
The trees tell tales at end of day.
A leaf once teased a passing breeze,
"Catch me if you can, if you please!"

The oak bark chuckled, feeling fine,
"Tell me your woes, and I'll entwine."
While pines stood tall with needles sharp,
Composing tunes, a lovely harp.

A willow bent to tell a pun,
"Life's too short, go have some fun!"
The chestnut giggled, wrapped in green,
"I've got your back, I'm on the scene!"

Lullabies of nature weave,
Bringing joy to those who believe.
In gentle laughter, wisdom flows,
Among the trees, the humor glows.

The Language of Ripeness

In the orchard where giggles burst,
Fruits confess their secrets first.
A peach flirted with an apricot,
"Your fuzzy skin's what I forgot!"

Leaves rustle with a playful tune,
Under the watchful eye of the moon.
Cherries laugh with juicy delight,
Puns and jokes under the starlight.

Grapes gossip on the vine's embrace,
Each juicy tale a sweetened grace.
While plums parade in skins so round,
Silly dances all around abound.

In this grove, a vibrant spree,
Nature's comedy, wild and free.
With every crunch and every bite,
A fruity giggle steals the night.

Silent Stories of the Grove

In the grove where silence reigns,
Whispers stir amidst the grains.
A melon slips and takes a fall,
"Oops, my rind was much too tall!"

Oranges gossip in bright delight,
"Have you heard about that pear's flight?"
With apples grinning, sharing the scene,
"Decisions are tough when you're so green!"

Cider dreams of a daring spree,
As lemons plot their tangy decree.
Berries laugh with a cheeky grin,
As soft winds egg them on to spin.

Underneath the leafy spray,
Nature's antics come out to play.
In the stillness, laughter grows,
A tale of fruit that nobody knows.

Softly Spoken Harvests

In fields where colors just collide,
Harvests whisper, secrets slide.
Pumpkins giggle, round and plump,
"Count on me for any jump!"

Squash winks, saying, "I'll grow tall,
Just watch me stretch, I'll never stall!"
Corn ears chuckle, swaying free,
"Popcorn dreams are best with glee!"

With every rustle, stories spread,
Softly spoken as they tread.
Sweet potatoes in a big embrace,
Share their dreams in this vibrant space.

Under sunlight, laughter flows,
Nature's humor always shows.
In every harvest, joy intertwined,
Echoes of fun in every rind.

The Scent of Forbidden Truths

In a basket of secrets, fruits conspire,
Whispers mingle, hearts desire.
A blueberry blurted alongside a pear,
"Voyage of flavor, do you dare?"

Plucking thoughts from boughs so high,
Crisp laughter floats like clouds in July.
The scent of mischief fills the air,
With every bite of fruity affair.

Lemons spill their sour tales,
Cherries burst, no need for veils.
While ripe banter weaves through the trees,
Fruitful secrets carried on the breeze.

In this world of zests and cheer,
Each flavor dances, loud and clear.
With hidden truths and jokes untold,
Fruity laughter never grows old.

Secrets of the Core

In the tree, a secret hides,
With leaves that giggle as it glides.
A worm with dreams of flying high,
He tried the wind, but oh, my, my!

The apples laugh, a cheeky crew,
Spinning stories, wild and new.
They plot and prank the tending hands,
While squirrels dance in mischief bands.

Whispers of the Orchard

The breeze, a giggle through the apple boughs,
Tickles the blossoms, it knows just how.
A toad sings karaoke on a rock,
While bees break dance and start to flock.

Oh, what a hoot, this orchard fest!
The fruits are jesters, who laugh the best.
Each branch a stage, each root a fan,
The harvest's humor, a merry plan!

Silent Autumn Calls

Autumn slips in with a cheeky grin,
Donning a cloak made of colors thin.
The pumpkins giggle at their own fate,
While acorns gossip, it's never too late!

Leaves tumble down like clumsy clowns,
Painting the ground with russet gowns.
Whispering secrets of harvest fun,
As the orchard sings 'til day is done!

Beneath the Fruitful Veil

Under the branches where shadows play,
The fruits exchange jokes throughout the day.
A pear told a pun that struck the core,
While cherries chuckled, wanting more!

With every breeze, the laughter swells,
As apples spin tales and weave their spells.
The ground rolls over with mirth so bright,
In the orchard's depths, pure delight!

A Dream Wrapped in Foliage

In a tree of green, dreams reside,
With giggles and whispers they often confide.
Leaves giggle as they sway in the breeze,
Sharing secrets with the bees.

Shiny and round, a jester so bright,
Hiding inside, a comical sight.
With a grin on its face, it begs to be seen,
Inviting all to join in its dream.

Silly songs flow from branches above,
Mary and Tom start sharing their love.
But with every bite, the laughter grows loud,
As juice dribbles down, it feels rather proud.

With each little crunch, the fun seems to rise,
As orchard critters join in the surprise.
So here in the grove, let laughter take flight,
Wrapped in foliage, all feels just right.

The Riddle Inside the Skin

What lies beneath this shiny façade?
A riddle wrapped up in a sweet charade.
Winking at squirrels from branches up high,
It chuckles aloud as passersby cry.

A peel to uncover, a puzzle to crack,
One bite, and you'll find the jokes all stack.
Sweetness and tartness collide in delight,
Leaving sticky fingers, a true candy fight.

Oh, the giggles from critters who take a taste,
It's a race to the core, no time to waste.
Each munch brings a riddle, each crunch brings a laugh,
While the juice makes a splash in this comical gaffe.

So gather your friends, join in the fun,
With riddles and flavors, there's joy for everyone.
The orchard's the stage, the trees are the clowns,
And laughter rings out in delightful sounds.

Crimson Secrets

In a patch of red under the sun's gold,
Secrets are whispered, sweet and bold.
Crimson orbs giggle with mischievous flair,
Sharing their tales with the warm summer air.

A bite into juicy, a splash of surprise,
The taste of summer's laughter, oh how it flies!
With sticky red lips, a story unfolds,
As secrets of sweetness begin to be told.

They roll down the hill, each one a delight,
Chasing each other, a comical sight.
With seeds like confetti, they laugh as they fall,
Celebrating their life, let's join in the call!

So come to the grove, let's dance and sing,
With crimson secrets, it's joy we'll bring.
Laughter and flavor, they twirl hand in hand,
In this world of wonder, let's make our stand!

Orchard Serenade

Under the boughs where the laughter grows,
A serenade plays, everyone knows.
The fruit of the day grins wide and bright,
As jokes float around in pure delight.

Tickled by breezes, they swing and sway,
Each tiny nibble makes worries decay.
Pink cheeks exploding with each juicy bite,
It's a fruit-fueled party, oh what a sight!

Bouncing and bouncing, they fall with a cheer,
Creating sweet music for all who come near.
With seeds as maracas, they shake with glee,
The orchard's alive with a comical spree.

So gather your friends for a merry parade,
Under the sunshine, let laughter cascade.
In this fruity festival, joy is the plan,
As we revel together, fruit lovers we stand!

Echoes Beneath the Fruit

Underneath the boughs, they crack jokes,
While sneaky squirrels dance like folks.
A riddle posed by the fruit so bright,
Laughter gathers, a comical sight.

With a wink, the berries join in play,
"What's green and red?" they shout, "Hooray!"
Beneath the leaves, chuckles take flight,
As giggles mingle with sunlight.

Even the wind has a thing to say,
Whistling tunes that make birds sway.
Tickling apples in the tree so wide,
Joy echoes forth, can't let it hide.

The worms all wiggle with delight,
As they enjoy this silly night.
In this grove, where laughter grows,
Every fruit knows how humor flows.

Silent Songs of the Grove

In a sunny glade, the pears all hum,
While cherries giggle, oh, what fun!
Peaches sway in a silly tune,
Under the watch of a bright silver moon.

A crabapple sings with a teasing tease,
"You think you're ripe? Just wait, please!"
Bananas snicker from their leafy helm,
Giggling softly, they take the realm.

Each pit has a tale, each skin a rhyme,
Jokes told by the pines, in perfect time.
"Who's the fool who can't get it straight?"
They chortle and chuckle, it's never late.

With every rustle, secrets are spun,
In the grove where the laughter's begun.
Under the stars, the garden sways,
As fruit holds court on funny days.

Stories Within a Seed

Within the seed, tales twist and twine,
A story of puns that are simply divine.
Out pops a sprout with a grin so wide,
Announcing, "Wait till you see my pride!"

A grape once joked, "I'm in quite a jam,"
With a berry burst, out came the slam!
Laughter erupts from the vine and blue,
Silly shenanigans in every hue.

An orange pip told a corny jest,
"I peel away worries, I'm simply the best!"
The laughter ripples through every leaf,
Spreading joy like a funny chief.

As they grow, the stories collide,
Funny adventures we can't betide.
Nature's stand-up, ripe with glee,
Unfolds each tale for all to see.

Awakened by the Fruit

Awake with a laugh, the fruit stretches wide,
With zest and glee, they cannot hide.
The morning sun tickles with rays,
As giggles sprout on fresh, bright days.

The lemons exclaim, "We're sour with zest!"
While boys prank the pears, just like a jest.
Bananas slip on their own peels, too,
A fruit-filled day just has to ensue.

A fig tells the tale of a mischievous ant,
Who claimed he could dance like a gallant plant.
With every twirl, the berries burst free,
For the wonder of fruit is a sight not to see.

The orchard joins in with a quirky display,
Where laughter and fun keep worries at bay.
So here's to the jesters in nature's fine loot,
Awakened by joy, every day's a hoot!

The Prelude of Ripeness

In the orchard, fruits conspire,
Giggles echo, no one's a liar.
Pies in dreams, sweet temptations,
Jokes about their juicy creations.

Red and green wearing a crown,
Swapping tales of falling down.
"I tripped over a worm!" said one,
"Not as funny as the squirrel who runs!"

Juicy laughter fills the air,
Fruits roll over without a care.
Each bump and bounce, a prank they play,
As the sun begins to sway.

So here's to the orchard's delight,
Where laughter ripens, day and night.
In a world where fruits just jest,
Their tales of joy— oh, they're the best!

Encounters with the Silent

In the twilight, shadows blend,
Fruits gossip without an end.
A pear, a peach, in quiet talks,
Plotting mischief as the sun walks.

"You won't believe who got juiced!"
Said the plum, feeling quite goosed.
"It was the banana, slipped and fell!"
And laughter spread, all hearts swell.

Amidst the still, the giggles swell,
Each wink a story they can tell.
A fruit's silent laugh is loud,
Leaving all the trees quite proud.

As night creeps in, the moon appears,
They share their dreams, their fruity cheers.
In silence, joy rings bright and true,
An orchard filled with laughter's hue.

Aroma of Silent Yearning

Fragrant wishes rise and swirl,
Tasting dreams in a fruit-filled whirl.
A banana blushes, feeling bold,
Tickled by tales that never get old.

Cherry dreams of midnight pranks,
While lemon joins the fruity ranks.
"Ever tried to catch a breeze?"
Laughter erupts with such great ease.

Juicy aromas float on high,
As fruit still yearns and wonders why.
A melon sighs with a secret laugh,
Longing for a funny photograph.

With every giggle, scents entwine,
In this garden, all is divine.
So here's to the fruit that dares to dream,
In silence, they flourish, a whimsical team.

The Call of Mellowing

As fruits grow soft, they start to sway,
Old tales surface in a playful way.
A ripe banana winks in delight,
"A softening story, hold on tight!"

Peaches, round and fuzzy, hold court,
Each one spinning a mellow retort.
"Ever seen a grape do a jig?"
They roll and giggle, feeling so big.

The air filled with sweetness and glee,
Fruits dancing together, carefree.
Laughter echoes through branches tall,
The call of sweet murmurs, enchanting all.

Mellow moments beneath the sky,
Fruity friends with a bashful sigh.
In this orchard, the world slows down,
With laughter rippling, all wear a crown!

Echoes in the Orchard

In an orchard bright and spry,
Fruits conspire as they roll by.
One said, "I'm the juiciest here!"
The others laughed, "Oh dear, oh dear!"

A worm slipped by, with a cheeky grin,
"I prefer the core, that's where I win!"
The fruits all giggled, what a sight!
Debates and jests took off in flight.

A bird chirped loud from up above,
"Let's dance and sing, oh peaches, love!"
They swayed and twirled with quite a cheer,
Making juice, spreading laughter here!

But then a basket came around,
"Oh no, oh no! We're homeward bound!"
Yet still they laughed, and what a feast,
In the end, it's joy — at least!

Beneath the Boughs

Beneath the boughs where shadows play,
A cider keg rolled in today.
"What's this?" yelled Pear with a loud clap,
"An apple party! Come take a nap!"

They tumbled in, they danced around,
Each fruit hip-hop, bouncing on the ground.
"This juice is good!" cried Granny Smith,
"Let's toast to summer, with a twist!"

Then cherry blurted, "Life's a peach!"
While lemons plotted — a prank, to teach.
In playful whispers, mischief brewed,
Till all went wild, cheers ensued!

As night draped down in moon's embrace,
They made sweet sauce, a sticky place.
With laughter echoing, oh what fun!
All fruits united, till the day was done!

The Language of Harvest

The harvest moon was glowing bright,
Each fruit expressed its pure delight.
"A party's coming! Let's take a chance!"
The apples laughed and started to dance.

Pumpkin grinned, "I'll be the king!"
While plums prepared a joyful fling.
"Let's roll around the patch with glee!"
"Who brings the punch?" they shouted in spree.

A friendly chatter filled the air,
Crispy leaves fell without a care.
With every joke, the spirits soared,
Each bite of fun, they all adored.

As laughter echoed 'neath the trees,
They feasted on pies, and shared the peas.
With every giggle, the night grew old,
In harvest's warmth, pure joy to behold!

Rustling Leaves of Wisdom

Rustling leaves whispered tales so sly,
Of fruit debates 'neath the bright sky.
"Why so juicy?" asked the grape,
"Because I'm sweet, and that's no drape!"

A seed spoke up, "You're all too ripe!
Try being funny, that's where the hype!"
The fruits all chuckled, tempers eased,
Wisdom sprouted as they teased.

"Let's make a punch with zest!" cried lime,
"Or blend a smoothie, oh what a crime!"
The orchard echoed with laughter tight,
In this quirky, fruity delight.

So when you wander where fruits convene,
Remember the laughter, it's evergreen.
For every fruit has a role to play,
In the comedy of life, they find their way!

Echoes of Forgotten Harvests

In the orchard, giggles soar,
Fruits hang low, daring a score.
A squirrel steals the show, keen,
While the apples plot, unseen.

Juicy jokes on branches sway,
Each bite, a game of ballet.
Laughter ripens, juicier still,
As shadows dance on the hill.

Old roots whisper stories wise,
Beneath the sun, each secret lies.
Pranks of the past, so absurd,
In the rustling leaves, they're heard.

When harvest time spills with glee,
Baskets piled high, what a spree!
With every crunch, a chuckle shared,
A feast of fun, none are scared.

Serenade of Ripening Fruit

In the breeze, the fruit's delight,
Chortles echo, day turns night.
Bouncing balls of red and green,
Twisting vines, an acrobatic scene.

With each tickle from a vine,
Nature's joke, a clever sign.
The pear winks as plums play coy,
Together, they invent new joy.

Caterpillars dance and tease,
Giving trees a chance to sneeze.
Honeybees hum a jolly tune,
While waiting for the afternoon.

They gather round, the fruits unite,
Telling tales that spark delight.
In this orchard, laughter's a must,
A fruity world, in glee we trust.

Hushed Tales in Green Leaves

Amidst the green, mischief swirls,
Leaves giggle while the tree twirls.
With a rustle, secrets spill,
Whispered tales of laughs and thrill.

Little bugs with hats parade,
Wobbling through the sunlight's shade.
Creating chaos, much to see,
As fruit joins in, a jubilee!

The breeze carries their hearty cheer,
Birds join in, perched without fear.
A ripe banana cracks a grin,
As mushrooms wink, let the game begin!

From roots to tips, the joy conceives,
Tickling thoughts in playful leaves.
In nature's pub, the fun won't cease,
These whispered smiles bring such peace.

Gifts from the Tree of Knowledge

Wisdom looms from branches high,
As laughter blooms beneath the sky.
An apple rolls, a playful ruse,
Spreading giggles with each bruise.

The elders chuckle, tales unfold,
Of little fruits, both brave and bold.
They craft a story, sweet and tart,
Unraveling the secrets of the heart.

Each nibble holds a curious jest,
As nature's wisdom put to test.
The trees conspire, plotting glee,
Inviting all, come taste with me!

And with each bite, a chuckle flows,
Gifts of knowledge, laughter grows.
In orchards vast, where jokes don't tire,
The spirit of fun ignites the fire!

Lurking Beneath the Surface

A fruit lay low on garden's floor,
With secrets ripe, it started to snore.
An ant walked by, then took a peek,
"Is this a dream or a fruit so sleek?"

The worms held meetings, oh what a sight,
Plotting to steal a bite by night.
They giggled and laughed, planning their feast,
While the apple just lay there, calm and increased.

A crow swooped down, quite out of breath,
"Did something move—or is it death?"
The fruit just rolled, and played along,
Honking away, like a duck with a song.

Yet all was well in this zany grove,
The fruit became a treasure trove.
Each creature chuckled, played a small part,
Life's little joys right from the heart.

The Aroma of Untold Tales

A scent wafted over the sunny glade,
Where gnomes in pajamas began to parade.
They sniffed and snorted, what could it be?
"Is it cake, perhaps? Or the smell of a tree?"

A wise old squirrel sat up in a sage,
"Might be the breath of a fruit on a stage."
He twiddled his thumbs, and rolled his eyes,
"Or maybe just donuts in glorious size!"

The fairies flew by, in dresses so bright,
"Let's taste the flavor; it's pure delight!"
They danced on the breeze, sprinkling sweet cheer,
As whispers of flavor brought all creatures near.

So in the shade, where stories run wild,
A fruit shared its secrets with laughter compiled.
No lesson or moral, just joy on the way,
Life's simple pleasures, let's savor today!

Whispers of Sweet Temptation

A juicy orb on a high tree branch,
Spoke softly, "Come, take a chance!"
The raccoons giggled, in masks of delight,
"Is it you who sings in the still of the night?"

The birds all gathered, keen for a chat,
"Could we take a bite, or even a spat?"
They fluttered about, in pecking demand,
"Just one little nibble, oh isn't it grand?"

Then the wind burst forth, like a jester's jest,
"Who wants to taste? It's nature's best!"
The fruit chuckled back, "I'm not your mate,
But go on, my friends, don't wait too late!"

With laughter and sparks, the banter went round,
As the fruit kept chatting without making a sound.
Just a stage full of jesters, and friends all around,
In a world where the sweet whispered joy ever found.

The Allure of Hidden Truths

Beneath the leaves, in the warm sunlight,
There thrived a tale that danced with delight.
A fruit wore a cloak, so shiny and bright,
"Who will discover my secrets tonight?"

A bumblebee buzzed, with a curious flick,
"Did you bloat on gossip, or learn a new trick?"
The fruit just winked, in a cheeky array,
"Why not pull me down and come out to play?"

The hedgehogs all squealed, with snorts and with glee,
"We'll roll you around, then see what we see!"
With snickers and snorts, they revved up their game,
While the fruit just chuckled, "You're all quite the same!"

With the moon shining bright, and the stars all aglow,
The laughter of creatures, a delightful show.
No truths left unspoken, just whispers of fun,
In the world of the sprightly, where mischief's begun.

Murmurs of Nature's Delight

In the garden, fruits start to grin,
Bouncing smiles on branches, what a win!
Bumblebees buzz with a silly cheer,
As a tomato quips, "Hey, I'm here!"

The daisies giggle in the summer breeze,
While a wise old tree tells jokes with ease.
"Knock knock! Who's there? Oh, just some dew!"
Nature's laughter, a joyful view!

Cherries are blushing, their cheeks so red,
"Don't you dare drop me!" a peach once said.
Mangoes swing in their sunlit glee,
As oranges dance, wild and free!

Under the moon, the veggies prance,
Cauliflower leads a wobbly dance.
Whispers of joy fill the starry night,
In this playful world, everything's bright!

Conversations of Color

A purple grape said, "What a delight!"
While a carrot laughed, "I'm such a sight!"
Green beans teased the red bell's flair,
"You make our salad look debonair!"

The yellow corn sang a sunny tune,
As broccoli twirled under the moon.
Eggplants chuckled with their smooth skin,
"With colors like these, we're bound to win!"

Radishes whispered, "Let's spice it up!"
While strawberries giggled from their cup.
Potatoes rolled, all muddy and bold,
"We're the stars, let the flavors unfold!"

Lettuce laughed, fluffed up in style,
A cabbage winked with its leafy smile.
In this garden of words, they share and play,
A colorful chat to brighten the day!

Ripened Realities

A quirky fig wore a hat so sly,
"Look at me!" it said, reaching for the sky.
Bananas slipped and started to laugh,
"We're the best! Let's take a photograph!"

Pineapples puffed, so proud and bold,
"We're the jewels of the tropical gold!"
A coconut chimed in with a grin,
"No need to worry, let the fun begin!"

Ripe avocados slayed with raps so fine,
"Slice us up! We're feeling divine!"
While watermelons rolled with a splash,
"Juicy and funny, oh what a bash!"

Under the sun, they shared a dream,
A fruit fiesta with laughter's theme.
In this orchard of jovial glee,
Life ripens well, just wait and see!

A Chorus of Seasons

In springtime's chat, flowers start to hum,
"Here comes the sun!" a daffodil's drum.
Tulips winked and twirled around,
While daisies danced on the soft ground.

Summer joined with a loud parade,
Berries burst, in tasty cascade.
"Catch us if you can!" the plums called out,
As the sun laughed bright, twirling about!

Autumn arrived with a harvest call,
Crispy leaves crunched, a colorful ball.
"Let's play in piles!" yelled a giddy pear,
As pumpkins giggled from everywhere.

Winter whispered in chilly tones,
"Frost is here; let's chill to our bones!"
Yet beneath the snow, a secret lies,
Life sleeps, ready for spring's reprise!

The Guardian of the Orchard

In the orchard, under trees,
A squirrel's dance brings me to tease.
He wears a cap, quite out of place,
While juggling apples with silly grace.

The branches shake, the leaves all sway,
As he drops one, oh, what a display!
The ground erupts in giggles and glee,
Even bees buzz with laughter, you see.

A rabbit hops to join the fun,
Says he'll race, but won't be outrun.
But with one puff of the fluffy tail,
He tumbles down, his pride set to bail.

I chuckle softly, watching the show,
Nature's clowns putting on a show.
In this garden, laughter won't fade,
Guardian of this chaos parade.

Rustle of Sweet Nothings

The leaves are chatting, what do they say?
About the gardener's clumsy day.
He tripped on roots with socks all bright,
And danced a jig that gave us delight.

A breeze comes through with a cheeky wink,
It tickles the branches, makes them rethink.
Sweet whispers float, a fruit's lively jest,
'Let's play hide and seek, who's the best?'

Under the boughs, I spy a pear,
He's got a hat, a dapper affair.
He grins wide, says, 'I'm the king, you see!'
But his hat's too big, it covers his glee.

The giggles spread, like pollen in spring,
These moments simple make the heart sing.
Rustling leaves, filled with life's little dreams,
In this orchard, all's bursting at the seams.

Nature's Gentle Murmurs

In the garden, whispers glide,
A ladybug's secret, she cannot hide.
'Trouble afoot!' she chirps with cheer,
As a worm wriggles, chasing a deer.

The daisies chuckle, their petals all bright,
They tease the sun, who's shining too light.
'Oh dear!' says Clover, 'We're all a bit lost,
But let's not forget the fun to be tossed!'

The frisky bunny hops in a jig,
Makes the shy daisies all dance a gig.
A breeze shushes, with stories to share,
Nature's whispers that bounce everywhere.

So come join the laughter, let spirits burst,
In this garden, no frown's ever cursed.
For amidst the giggles and soft murmur sounds,
Life's gentle prance always astounds.

In the Shade of Sweetness

In the shade, where the sun can't peep,
A sleepy bug chuckles, 'I need some sleep.'
But a rascal crow with a pranking eye,
Sneaks up and shouts, 'Wake up! Don't be shy!'

The berries giggle, red cheeks aglow,
While the grapes join in with a little toe show.
They roll and tumble, all in a heap,
Making the sleepybug laugh till he weeps.

A gentle breeze joins the playful parade,
Spinning the leaves, the colors invade.
Under this canopy, dreams come alive,
With each tickle of laughter, more joy can thrive.

The day drifts on, in a sugary haze,
Creating sweet moments, in playful displays.
In this orchard's shade, life's never a bore,
With whispers of fun, forever we explore.

Orchard's Lullaby

In soft leaves' rustle, secrets sway,
A squirrel tries to steal my tray.
The branches dance with every breeze,
While crickets play their nighttime tease.

The fruit hangs low and shines so bright,
A worm's debate on which to bite.
The laughter of the trees is clear,
As birds join in with songs sincere.

A picnic spreads, the blanket's frayed,
We juggle fruit, and yes, we've strayed.
With every crunch, a giggle shared,
In this sweet haven, none is scared.

Oh, say, what fun beneath the sun,
With nature's snacks, we laugh and run.
We munch on joy, refresh the parts,
In playful bounty, life imparts.

Seeds of Memory

In the middle of a crunch parade,
I drop my snack, it's quite the trade.
The ants arrive, a marching band,
As if they've heard my berry stand.

With every bite, a story grows,
Like sticky tales in sweet, red prose.
A seed I planted quite by chance,
Now dances forth in juice-filled prance.

A cider spill leads to a slip,
A twirling dive from my tight grip.
My friends all laugh, we roll and play,
In fruity chaos, we'll stay all day.

Each moment ripe, a press of time,
In apple laughter, we unwind.
With giggles pressed inside the core,
Our seeds of memory grow evermore.

A Symphony in Red

The orchard hums a tasty tune,
As apples jest beneath the moon.
They twirl and spin in jolly cheer,
While we all chase them without fear.

A plucky fruit begins to roll,
And off it goes, it has a goal!
With each soft thud and comical fall,
We're giggling loud; you hear the call?

In ruby glory, we sway and laugh,
As chunks of pie become our staff.
Each slice a note, a tune so clear,
A joyous feast that we hold dear.

The orchard sings with zest and zing,
Where apples play and laughter spring.
With every bite, a symphony,
In cheeky crunches, wild and free.

Reveries of the Picking Hand

With each small stretch, I reach so high,
To grab a treat, I cannot lie.
A silly flop, I tumble down,
My hat a crown turned upside down.

The juiciest fruit, a treasure bright,
Decisions made in pure delight.
But oh, beware the cheeky breeze,
That steals my prize with crafty ease!

In daydreams filled with apple pie,
I pluck, I twirl; the time flies by.
A jester's game in grassy glades,
As giggles burst in fruity parades.

With baskets full, our hands outstretched,
We dance and laugh, all plans bewitched.
In harvest's joy, we share our glee,
A perfect day for you and me.

Whispers of Autumn's Bounty

In the crisp air, critters play,
Squirrels dance, a jolly ballet.
They scurry and scamper with glee,
Trying to steal their feast for free.

Pumpkins grin with a cheeky glance,
While apples giggle, causing a dance.
"You can't catch me!" they shout in cheer,
As wind swirls laughter, crisp and clear.

Jugs of cider line up in rows,
Like old friends teasing, everyone knows.
"Take a sip and spin around,
You'll find yourself on spinny ground!"

So fill your basket with silly fruits,
They'll tickle your toes and tie your boots.
Autumn's laughter, round every bend,
A harvest joke that will never end.

Delicate Temptations

A fruit so bright, a fabled prize,
With sparkly skin and teasing lies.
"Take a bite!" they softly chime,
But shares of mischief taste divine!

Cherries giggle, red and round,
While pears disguise in leafy gown.
"Pick me, pick me!" the blueberries sing,
As wise old grapes say, "What a fling!"

Plums making puns in smooth, sweet tone,
Comedians in fruit, all on their own.
"Life's too short, come join the fun,
With sugary laughs, together we run!"

Bananas slip with playful charm,
With every grin, they cause alarm.
Fruits unite, in sweet delight,
In a comedic bowl, it feels so right.

Shadows in the Fruit Basket

In a dark corner, two apples plot,
Swinging advice from the ripened lot.
"Let's play hide and seek tonight,
Under the moon, in the silver light!"

Bananas watch, they peel with glee,
"Don't get too cozy, or you might see!"
Pineapples snicker with prickly laughs,
At peeking lemons and their other halves.

"Who's the sweetest?" they ponder aloud,
"Oh my, we're all so well-endowed!"
With fruity secrets and juicy lore,
Even tarts toss in one-liners galore.

Then comes the night, shadow games ensue,
A sly laughter, a berry or two.
In the basket, the fun takes flight,
Tales of fruit, in the dark of night.

The Taste of Untold Stories

Gather 'round, fruits from afar,
Sharing tales beneath the stars.
Slice of lemon, sharp as a thumb,
Sour tales that make everyone hum.

Oranges strain, a zest-filled fable,
Turning giggles into a fable.
"Juicy gossip" is made to share,
While cherries bounce in mischievous flair.

A fruitroll of rhymes, they pass the time,
With every slice, they create a rhyme.
Peaches blush at a hilarious pun,
In the world of fruit, there's mounds of fun!

So bring your basket, let's join the feast,
With humor fresh, we'll never cease.
For in each bite, a laugh awaits,
In every fruit, untold debates.

Conversations in the Air

In the orchard, gossip flies,
Fruits all chat beneath blue skies.
"Who's the juiciest?" Apple grins,
While Pear just rolls her eyes and spins.

"Watch that worm," a Banana shouts,
"His stories? Full of twists and clouts!"
"Try a scoop of my sweet jam,"
Said Apricot with playful slam.

"Life's a breeze with nature's crew,
Grab a slice; it's all for you!"
Laughing leaves, they dance, they play,
Who knew fruit could steal the day?

Beneath branches, shadows cast,
"We're ripe today, let's have a blast!"
Their fruity banter, quite bizarre,
Turns the orchard into a star!

Secrets of the Ripened

In the corner, a secret is brewed,
A stashed apple, his thoughts construed.
Hiding tales of trips gone wrong,
"My cider's strong, but don't sing my song!"

Strawberry whispers, "I swear, you'll see,
These apples think they run the spree!"
Then Kiwi chimes with a smirk on his face,
"Just wait 'til they taste my sweet embrace!"

Peach bursts in with bravado, it's clear,
"Who needs a mirror? I am the sphere!"
Grapes just giggle, their vines intertwined,
"Let's keep our juiciest stories confined!"

As sunlight dips, secrets unfold,
In this fruity world, bold tales are told.
Laughter ripens amid the leaves,
The joy of secrets, nothing deceives.

Beneath the Pink Veil

Under blossoms, giggles arise,
Petals falling, sweet surprise.
"Don't drop too low!" a Cherry squeaks,
As Breezy winds play hide and seek.

Pink veils sway, just shade for fun,
"Bet you can't catch me!" said one.
Peach rolled away, in playful haste,
Leaving behind a cheeky taste.

Grapes peek out, their clusters tight,
"Who needs a crown? We rule the night!"
A raspberry sighs, "I'm just too sweet,
But humor's what makes me complete!"

So let the blossoms twirl and dance,
In this fruity world, take a chance.
Below the pink, all is bright,
With laughter carrying through the night.

Dreaming in Orchard Hues

Underneath the twilight's glow,
Fruits whisper dreams of high and low.
"What if we painted the sky with zest?"
"Or turned the clouds into a fruit fest?"

Mango dreams of a sunny parade,
While Plum suggests a fruit charade.
"Let's wear colors, wild and free,
I'll be orange; who wants to be?"

The night thickens, ideas swell,
"Let's wake the stars!" a Kiwi yells.
Imaginary treats fall from above,
In this orchard, arched with love.

So let us toast, in grape-filled cheer,
To dreams that blossom all year near.
In hues of laughter, joy, and fun,
Together we shine, and life's just begun!

Plucked from Perception

In a garden so bright and green,
Lies a fruit of a wacky sheen.
It giggles as you take a bite,
Causing joy and pure delight.

Falling from branches with a thud,
It lands right in a puddle of mud.
Splashing all the ants nearby,
They march away with a squeaky sigh.

Its skin so shiny, smooth, and bold,
Tells secrets of legends long told.
A crunch so loud it makes you jump,
Perhaps it's really just a grump!

With every nibble, laughter flows,
As silly jokes the apple knows.
So grab a slice and let it roll,
For fun is buried in its soul.

Memories in Each Bite

Beneath the sun, the orchard beams,
Each fruit holds more than just our dreams.
A nibble takes you back in time,
Where fruit punch parties were sublime.

With every crunch, a laugh erupts,
As silly stories get unwrapped.
A core that tells of days so bright,
Like sticky fingers, all in sight.

The fruit of knowledge, so they say,
But this one just wants to play.
Tell a joke, and watch it grin,
With every bite, joy's sure to win.

So munch away, don't hesitate,
Each flavor's like a song or fate.
With every slice, the giggles start,
For memories live in the heart!

The Hidden Voice of the Tree

Up high a tree, it starts to sing,
A melody of the silliest thing.
Branches sway with whispers anew,
What secrets lie in a fruity brew?

Leaves rustle soft, with laughter so spry,
As nuts and fruits all say goodbye.
They drop with giggles, a fruity parade,
Causing a ruckus in the glade.

The trunk, it chuckles, a warm embrace,
As squirrels dance at a frantic pace.
"Aren't we funny?" they seem to squeak,
While munching morsels and playing hide-and-seek.

So listen close to nature's quirk,
For every fruit and nut does smirk.
In every sound, a playful tease,
A hidden joy in every breeze.

Branches of Secrets

In branches high, where shadows play,
Secrets of laughter come out to stay.
The fruits all giggle, with tales to spin,
Of times when laughter was a win.

Pears joke with plums, a fruit buffoon,
Underneath a carefree moon.
While berries prance in a colorful dance,
Waltzing freely, given the chance.

"Hey, I'm delicious!", one fruit claims,
While apples join in the silly games.
A fruit fight breaks out, it's quite absurd,
As laughter erupts, it's truly heard.

So climb up high and join the fun,
In orchards where memories run.
Among the branches, joy takes flight,
With every fruit, a giggly bite.

Threads of Nature's Discourse

In the orchard, tales unfold,
Fruitful gossip, bright and bold.
A pear jokes, 'I'm better, see?'
'Only if you're not on my tree!'

The carrots laugh, 'We're on the ground!'
'Though underground, we're quite renowned!'
While apples chuckle, 'We shine on top!'
'But it's us roots that make you hop!'

Beneath the sky, the chat persists,
With snickers shared, no fruit resists.
The wind carries their silly lore,
As nature's quirks make spirits soar!

So gather 'round, let joy take flight,
In the garden of laughter, day and night.
For every leaf has jokes to tell,
In this fruit-filled world where all is well!

The Allure of Bittersweet

A cherry sighed, 'Life's just a game,'
'When sour's sweet, who's to blame?'
Lemon grinned, 'I lend my zest!'
'Mix us up, we're truly blessed!'

From fuzzy peach to tangy lime,
They joke about the passing time.
'What's green and mean?' a melon teased,
'An avocado, waiting for ease!'

As fruit debates its rightful place,
With playful jabs and funny face.
A grapefruit claimed, 'I'm full of glee!'
'Tell that to your breakfast spree!'

The laughter rang from vine to tree,
In every fruit, a mystery.
So let's all taste the jests once more,
Bittersweet flavors we all adore!

Grappling with Growth

A sprout yelled, 'Watch me shoot up fast!'
'You're just a weed, I'll outlast!'
The flower laughed, 'You're still so small!'
'Growing pains just make me ball!'

The pumpkin puffed, 'I'm round and proud!'
'But watch your leaves, they're way too loud!'
A sunflower winked with golden glow,
'You'll trip on roots, just take it slow!'

In this garden, all have flair,
With scuffles and tussles in the air.
A bittersweet tussle, fun and bright,
Each leaf chats on in pure delight!

So let the rivalry freely flow,
Through dirt and joy, learn as we grow.
With every giggle, plant your feet,
And make your struggle feel so sweet!

Quiet Cravings in the Breeze

A pear sighed, 'I crave a fall,
A cozy spot, not too tall!'
An apple smirked, 'Let's dance and twirl,
With every breeze our laughter's a whirl!'

'Let's swing on branches, take a chance!'
A cherry chirped, 'Join in the dance!'
They tickled the leaves, all gentle and shy,
As whispers floated softly by.

'Would you like a taste of my sweet delight?'
An orange grinned, 'I'm juicy and bright!'
But kiwi rolled its eyes, oh so sly,
'Let's skip the feast, just share a pie!'

In whispers and giggles, all take flight,
Cravings linger in the soft twilight.
With every breeze, desire gleams,
As fruit unites in wild, fun dreams!

Whispered Hues and Shades

In the orchard, fruits conspire,
With secrets shared that never tire.
A crimson grin, a greenish tease,
They giggle softly in the breeze.

One pear dressed up to steal the show,
While lemons laugh, a zesty glow.
A banana slips with a sly delight,
As mangoes plot a fruity flight.

A radish blinks in vibrant red,
While carrots boast of what they've spread.
With whispers shared from leaves to roots,
The harvest dance in quirky suits.

So next time when you stroll about,
Listen close, there's no doubt.
Fruits have jokes, they've got the flair,
In their world, we're just visitors there.

An Overture of Fruits

On a treetop, plums spin round,
In the melody of a silly sound.
An apple sings a funny tune,
As grapes all sway, a fruity croon.

A cheeky peach slips on a leaf,
While cherries giggle in disbelief.
A jolly fig munches on sweet air,
And all of them just love to share.

The berries burst in laughter loud,
As lemons form a sunny crowd.
Together they frolic, hop and play,
In this fruity opera, come what may.

An orange winks at the coconut's charm,
While kiwis grin with sunny warm.
Take a seat, you've got a front-row view,
This is the show for me and you!

The Art of Subtlety

With a wiggle here and a giggle there,
Fruits conspire with crafty flair.
A peach in disguise, a melon so sly,
They spin tales and wave goodbye.

A carrot whispers with a crunch,
While beets are plotting, soft in their hunch.
With leafy secrets shared with glee,
What funny fruits they all can be!

A refined radish acts quite bold,
While pumpkins trade jokes worth their weight in gold.
In this garden, laughter blooms,
As veggies escape their dinner's gloom.

Smooth avocados share rich delight,
Under a moon that's oh so bright.
Celebrate this quirky cheer,
In the garden where all fruits appear.

Relics of Harvest

In the fields where laughter grows,
Harvest tales from nature flows.
Tomatoes chuckle, squishy red,
As zucchinis make fun of what they said.

Potatoes roll with a hearty laugh,
While onions team up to make a gaffe.
With carrots prancing in grand parade,
They're all the relics of a funny trade.

With pumpkins grinning, full of cheer,
They dance about, year after year.
And when the corn cackles with a twist,
You can bet a cob can't be missed!

These harvest relics, bold and bright,
Gifts of joy from morning light.
Next time you munch a crunch surprise,
Remember their laughter in disguise!

Murmurs of the Orchard

In the orchard where fruits do chat,
Gossip flows like a friendly cat.
Laughter echoes from tree to tree,
It's a fruity gala, come see and be free.

Juicy tales told with a grin,
Ripe reflections where fun begins.
Those brownish spots have secrets to share,
Like that one pear who thinks it's a millionaire!

A chorus of color, red through green,
Each fruit has a tale that's rarely seen.
Dancing shadows among the leaves,
Winking hues where mischief weaves.

So if you wander and catch a tune,
Listen closely, it might make you swoon.
The jests from the grove are quite absurd,
Even the worms giggle, haven't you heard?

Hidden Truths in Every Bite

Did you know that berries can sing?
Each crunch holds a secret like a spring.
A rascal peach with a fuzzy smile,
Claims he can dance down the aisle!

Grapes joke about their sour friends,
Bottled up laughter that never ends.
A cherry blinks, 'I'm the juiciest here!',
While apples chuckle, 'We have no fear!'

Galloping melons roll down the lane,
While strawberries giggle, 'Don't call us vain!'
Pick a fruit, take a big bite,
You might taste the laughter, it's quite a delight.

So feast on the fun that nature imparts,
With each juicy morsel, let joy fill your hearts.
For hidden truths and silly delights,
Are wrapped up in every fruit that excites.

Secrets of the Orchard's Heart

Deep in the grove where the rascals play,
Fruits share secrets in a quirky way.
A sneaky fig with a twinkle in sight,
Says laughter's the key to a fruitful night.

Plums in their coats, like little spies,
Trade tales of the breeze and gossip flies.
'Have you seen the apples, so shiny and proud?'
They flash their colors and whisper aloud.

Bananas peel back layers of doubt,
Claiming the throne, they raise a shout.
'We're the ripest joke in this playful scene,
With every slip, we're the comedy queens!'

So in the orchard, where cheer takes part,
You'll find the laughter that fills every heart.
For every fruit has a giggle to share,
Sprinkled with joy, floating in the air.

Lush Promises and Silent Sighs

In a riotous grove where the fruits convene,
They shout out loud, like a comedy scene.
Lemons laugh at the drama of life,
While berries tease, 'We've conquered all strife!'

A crisp little apple, bold and bright,
Makes claims of stardom that tickle the night.
While pears tumble down, with giggles and sighs,
They plot their escape under moonlit skies.

Watermelons jest as they bask in the sun,
Hiding their seeds, they're always the fun.
Each bite is a giggle, a chuckle, a cheer,
Fruits cracking jokes, come lend them your ear.

So join this party of colors and fun,
Where laughter blooms and worries are none.
The promises lush, wrapped in humor and cheer,
In this orchard of whispers, come gather near.

www.ingramcontent.com/pod-product-compliance
Lightning Source LLC
Chambersburg PA
CBHW070310120526
44590CB00017B/2610